English C2 Proficiency Vocab
The Most Important Words You need to
Pass all C2 Proficiency English Level Exams and
Tests

by CEP Publishing

2

English C2 Proficiency Vocabulary 2020 Edition: The Most Important Words You Need to Know to Pass all C2 Proficiency English Level Exams and Tests

by CEP Publishing

Introduction

This book contains all the most important words you need to know to pass all C2 Proficiency English level exams and tests.

This material is perfect for any serious candidate who does not wish to waste time researching and learning new vocabulary the traditional way. This book will make your learning more efficient with less of your own effort, which means more spare time to review other concepts.

This is not just a regular dictionary with a bunch of words. In this little vocabulary you can find only the most necessary C2 English level definitions. Knowing these words will help you pass all the relevant tests and exams, and will definitely surprise your examiner, in a good way.

Abstruse

Difficult to understand, especially when you think it could be explained more simply.

Acquisition

Means the process of getting or obtaining something (for example: The children progressed in the acquisition of basic skills).

Acrimonious

Marked by strong resentment or cynicism; someone or something is bitter or harsh in manner or speech, or rubs a person the wrong way.

Adage

Is a short, pointed, and memorable saying, which is considered a veritable truth by the majority of people; a traditional saying expressing a common experience or observation.

Adjure

Means to command solemnly; ask for or request earnestly; to order someone to do something.

Affectation

A deliberate pretense or exaggerated display; something that is not part of your personality but that you do to impress people.

Agile

When someone or something is agile, it can deal with changes quickly and successfully.

Akrasia

Is a state of mind in which someone acts against their better judgment through the "weakness of will."

Allure

Means the quality of being attractive, exciting, or interesting.

Allusion

Is a figure of speech that makes a reference to a place, person, or event. This can be real or imaginary and may refer to anything, including fiction, folklore, historical events, or religious manuscripts (for example: When she lost her job, she acted like a Scrooge, and refused to buy anything that wasn't necessary).

Ambiguous

Means unclear or vague in meaning; having more than one possible meaning.

Ambivalence

Is a state of having simultaneous conflicting reactions, beliefs, or feelings towards some object. Stated another way, ambivalence is the experience of having an attitude towards someone or something that contains both positive and negative components. The term also refers to situations where "mixed feelings" of a more general sort are experienced, or where a person experiences uncertainty or indecisiveness.

Amenable

Open and responsive to suggestion; easily persuaded or controlled.

Amend

Means to make minor changes to the text (piece of legislation, etc.) in order to make it more fair or accurate, or to reflect changing circumstances.

Aplomb

Unflappable self-possession, especially when in a difficult situation.

Apostasy

Is the act of giving up your religious or political beliefs and leaving a religion or a political party.

One who commits apostasy is known as an apostate.

Appease

Make peace with; pacify or placate (someone) by acceding to their demands (for example: She claimed that the government had only changed the law in order to appease their critics).

Apprise

Means to inform somebody of something (for example: We must apprise them of the dangers that may be involved).

Aquiver

Shaking or trembling slightly, often because of strong emotion (like while watching very tense moment in a movie).

Arcane

Requiring secret or mysterious knowledge; understood by few; mysterious or secret.

Archetype

Means something that is considered to be a perfect or typical example of a particular kind of person or thing, because it has all their most important characteristics (for example: The United States is the archetype of a federal society).

Arduous

Extremely difficult or hard, needing a lot of effort and energy (for example: An arduous climb; an arduous task).

Arid

Means extremely dry or deathly boring. If you describe something, such as a period of your life, as arid, you mean that it has so little interest, excitement, or purpose that it makes you feel bored or unhappy.

Arouse

To cause someone to have a particular feeling, or response; to cause an emotion or attitude.

Assertion

Is a statement, usually backed up by some kind of solid proof or reasoning; a confident and forceful statement of fact or belief.

Assiduous

Means persistent, hard-working. If you call someone assiduous, it means they're careful, methodical and very persistent.

Assuage

Means to make (an unpleasant feeling) less intense (for example: Nurse can assuage someone's pain with medication).

Assumption

Something that you consider likely to be true even though no one has told you directly or even though you have no proof.

Astute

Having the ability to accurately assess situations or people for one's own advantage.

Austere

Means stern and forbidding. If you describe something as austere, you approve of its plain and simple appearance.

Avail

To be of use, help, worth, or advantage (to), as in accomplishing an end (for example: My attempts to improve the situation were of little/no avail).

Avarice

Means greedy desire for wealth or material gain.

Backlog

Means a number of things which have not yet been done but which need to be done (for example: I've got a huge backlog of work to do).

Banter

Good-humored, playful conversation; the playful and friendly exchange of teasing remarks.

Bashful

Self-consciously timid, often feeling uncomfortable with other people and easily embarrassed.

Befuddle

To confuse; cause to become unable to think clearly.

Beguile

Means to persuade or trick someone into doing something, especially by saying nice things to them.

Bellicose

Inclined or ready to fight; aggressively hostile.

Belligerent

Aggressive and angry; aggressively hostile; pertaining to war or to those engaged in war.

Benevolent

Friendly and helpful; characterized by or expressing goodwill or kindly feelings.

Bewilder

To become perplexed and confused (for example: Beware of false people and situations that may bewilder you temporarily).

Bias

Means the action of supporting or opposing a particular person or thing in an unfair way or different from the way you treat other people.

Blare

Means to make a loud and unpleasant noise (for example: If something such as a siren or radio blares or if you blare it, it makes a loud, unpleasant noise).

Bombastic

Ostentatiously lofty in style; using words that are intended to impress people but do not sound sincere or do not express things very clearly.

Boon

Something that is desirable, favorable, or beneficial (for example: She told her husband that he owed her a boon).

Boondoggle

Work of little or no value done merely to look busy; an unnecessary and expensive piece of work.

Boorish

Rude; ill-mannered; not caring about other people's feelings.

Brackish

Means distasteful and unpleasant (for example: Brackish water is slightly salty and unpleasant).

Brazen

Obvious, without any attempt to be hidden. If you describe a person/behavior as brazen, you mean that they are very bold and don't care what other people think about them or their actions.

Brusque

Quick and rude in speech or manner; rudely abrupt, unfriendly.

Burgeon

To develop, expand, or grow rapidly (for example: Within a few weeks, the growth would burgeon into a huge cancer tumor).

Cadaverous

Having appearance or color of dead human body; looking very pale and ill.

Cajole

Means to persuade someone to do something by encouraging them softly or being good to them.

Camaraderie

The quality of affording easy familiarity and sociability; mutual trust and friendship among people who spend a lot of time together;

brotherhood, partnership, jovial unity, sociability amongst friends.

Canny

Clever and able to think quickly, especially in business or financial matters.

Cantankerous

Means ill humored, irritable, marked by ill-tempered contradiction or opposition, ugly, malicious.

Castigation

To criticize someone or something severely; verbal punishment. The word comes from the Latin castigus which means "to make pure".

Catharsis

Is the purging of the emotions, especially through certain kinds of art (as music or tragedy) that brings about spiritual renewal or release from tension.

Cavil

To raise irritating and trivial objections; to argue or protest about unimportant details.

Chide

Means to speak to someone brutally because they have behaved badly.

Choosy

Someone who is choosy has definite ideas about what they like and will not accept other things (for example: Choosy customers).

Circumlocution

Can be described as the use of too many words to say something, especially in order to avoid saying something clearly; an indirect way of expressing something.

Coercion

Means persuading someone to do something by using force or threats. In law, coercion is codified as a duress crime. Such actions are used as leverage, to force the victim to act in a manner that is contrary to their own interests.

Cogent

Reasonable and convincing; based on evidence; forcefully persuasive (for example: Cogent arguments; cogent evidence).

Coincide

Means to happen at or near the same time or during the same period, to occupy exactly the same space.

Compunction

Is a feeling of deep regret, usually for some misdeed (for example: I really have a compunction about helping to put your girlfriend into drama).

Concede

Means to admit or accept that something is true after first denying or resisting it.

Conciliation

Is the act of placating and overcoming distrust and animosity; the action or process of ending a disagreement.

Condescending

Showing or characterized by a patronizing or superior attitude toward others.

Confidant

Means someone to whom private matters are told. A confidant is the person you tell your secrets to.

Conformity

Is the act of matching attitudes, beliefs, and behaviors to group norms. This tendency to conforms to small groups and/or society as a whole, and may result from subtle unconscious influences, or direct and overpressure. Conformity can occur in the presence of others, or when an individual is alone.

Congruence

Is the consistency of different elements, objects, components of any structure, their harmonious work and consistency with each other, due to which harmonious work and integrity of the overall structure are achieved.

Connive

To plan secretly and dishonestly for something to happen; to form intrigues.

Connotation

Is a feeling or idea that is suggested by a particular word although it need not be a part of the word's meaning, or something suggested by an object or situation (for example, the word "lady" has connotations of refinement and excessive femininity that some women find offensive).

Construe

Make sense of; to understand the meaning, especially of other people's actions and statements, in a particular way.

Contention

The disagreement that results from opposing arguments; the act of competing as for profit or a prize.

Contravene

Go against, as of rules and laws.

Convergence

The state of separate elements joining or coming together (for example: If roads or paths converge, they move towards the same point where they join).

Conviction

Means a fixed or strong belief or opinion (for example: She takes pride in stating her political convictions).

Cosmopolitanism

Is the ideology that all human beings belong to a single community, based on a shared morality. A person who adheres to the idea of cosmopolitanism in any of its forms is called a cosmopolitan or cosmopolite.

Coterie

A group that meets socially; an exclusive circle of people with common purpose.

Countenance

Give sanction or support to; tolerate or approve
(for example: If someone will not countenance
something, they do not agree with it and will not
allow it to happen).

Credulous

Having a tendency to believe on slight evidence;
easily imposed upon; unsuspecting and very
gullible.

Culpable

Deserving blame or censure; responsible for doing
something bad or unlawful.

Curtail

Reduce in extent or quantity; terminate or abbreviate before its intended or proper end.

Daunting

Seeming difficult to deal with in prospect; making you feel slightly frightened or worried about your ability to achieve this (for example: A daunting task).

Dearth

Means scarcity, shortage of food, famine from failure or loss of crops.

Debase

Means to reduce the value, quality, or status of something (for example: War debases people).

Decimate

To kill or destroy a large number of something (for example: The Black Death decimated the army of the Kipchak khan Janibeg).

Deft

Very skillful, capable (for example: She's very deft at handling difficult situations).

Delectable

Delightful; delicious; extremely pleasing to the sense of taste.

Delineate

Portray; depict; draw or trace outline of; sketch out.

Delinquent

Means failing in duty, offending by neglect of duty. A delinquent person behaves in a way that is illegal or not acceptable to most people.

Demure

Shy or modest; quiet and well behaved.

Denigrate

To speak damagingly of; to criticize something in a way that shows you think it has no value/importance at all.

Denounce

Condemn openly; criticize; make known in formal manner.

Depute

Means transfer power to someone; appoint or instruct (someone) to perform a task for which one is responsible.

Deride

To criticize someone or something by suggesting that they are foolish or useless.

Derogatory

Showing strong disapproval and not showing respect.

Desecrate

To damage or show no respect towards something special, holy, or very much respected.

Deterrent

Means something immaterial that interferes with action or progress (for example: The stop sign on the corner is supposed to be a deterrent that discourages speeding).

Deviant

(from the Latin word deviare (meaning "to turn out of the way")) is a term used to describe a person or behavior that is not usual and is generally considered to be different and unacceptable.

Digression

The act of turning aside, straying from the main point, especially in a speech or argument.

Disclose

Expose to view as by removing a cover; to make something known publicly, or to show something that was hidden.

Disconsolate

Sad; cheerless; gloomy; hopeless or not expecting.

Discordant

Not in agreement or harmony (for example: Discordant note).

Disdain

Means to regard with scorn or contempt. If you disdain to do something, you do not do it, because you feel that you are too important to do it.

Disparage

Express a negative opinion of (for example: He never missed an opportunity to disparage his competitors).

Dispassionate

Able to be rational and make fair judgments or decisions that are not influenced by personal feelings or emotions.

Docile

Easily handled or managed; submissive; ready to accept control or instruction.

Doctrine

(from Latin doctrina (meaning "teaching, instruction")) is a belief or set of beliefs, especially political or religious ones that are taught and accepted by a particular group.

Dour

Means hard; inflexible; obstinate; gloomy in manner or appearance.

Ebullient

Overflowing with fervor, enthusiasm, or excitement; high-spirited.

Eclecticism

Is a combination of dissimilar, internally unrelated and possibly incompatible attitudes, ideas, concepts, styles, etc. The essence of eclecticism is the use of disparate elements to create something new.

Effrontery

Audacious behavior that you have no right to; extreme rudeness.

Egregious

Conspicuously and outrageously bad or reprehensible (for example: Egregious abuses of copyright).

Eloquent

Expressing what you mean using clear and effective language; fluent or persuasive in speaking or writing.

Elucidate

Means to explain something or make something clear.

Emancipation

Means any effort to procure economic and social rights, political rights or equality, often for a specifically disenfranchised group, or more generally, in the discussion of such matters.

Embellish

To decorate, to add details to, enhance.

Embezzle

Means to steal money/wealth that people trust you to look after.

Empirical

Means something that is based on investigation, observation, experimentation, or experience. If knowledge is empirical, it's based on observation rather than theory.

Enervate

Cause (someone or something) to feel drained of energy; weaken.

Enigma

Means a person or thing that is mysterious, puzzling, or difficult to understand.

Enmity

Is a feeling of strong dislike or hate (for example: There was an enmity between two warring countries).

Ennui

Is a feeling of being bored and having no interest in anything.

Epigram

Means a brief, interesting, memorable, and sometimes surprising or satirical statement; a short saying or poem which expresses an idea in a very clever and amusing way.

Epitaph (from Greek epitaphios (meaning "a funeral oration")) is a short text honoring a deceased person. Strictly speaking, it refers to text that is inscribed on a tombstone or plaque, but it may also be used in a figurative sense.

Epitome

Is the typical or highest example of a stated quality. If you say that a person or thing is the epitome of something, you are emphasizing that they are the best possible example of a particular type of person or thing (This hotel was the epitome of British colonial elegance in Jamaica; Maureen was the epitome of sophistication).

Equivocation

("calling two different things by the same name") is an informal fallacy resulting from the use of a particular word/expression in multiple senses throughout an argument leading to a false conclusion. For example:

"All jackasses have long ears."

"Carl is a jackass."

"Therefore, Carl has long ears."

Here, the equivocation is the metaphorical use of "jackass" to imply a simple-minded or obnoxious person instead of a male donkey.

Eschew

Deliberately avoid using; abstain from; avoid doing something (for example: Eschew violence).

Estimation

Means a rough calculation of the value, number, quantity, or extent of something (for example: Our team is requesting estimates from several companies to get an idea of the project cost).

Euphemism

(from Greek euphemia (meaning "the use of words of good omen")) is a polite word or expression that is used to refer to taboo topics (such as disability, sex, excretion, and death). For example, "passed away" is a euphemism for "died". It also may be a replacement of a name or a word that could reveal secret or holy and sacred names to the uninitiated.

Exacerbation

The process of making some problem, disease, or bad situation that is already bad even worse.

Exaggeration

Is a representation of something in an excessive manner. People exaggerate things because they have strong feelings about something. People may exaggerate to make people listen to what they say. They may do it to emphasize something. They may also exaggerate just to sound funny.

Exemplify

To be or give a typical example of something (for example: This painting perfectly exemplifies the western style).

Extemporize

Perform or speak without preparation (for example: I'd lost my notes and had to extemporize).

Extrapolate

In general, it means using facts about the present or about one thing or group to make a guess about the future or about other things or groups. When you extrapolate, you use specific details to make a general conclusion. For example, if you travel to Canada and encounter only friendly, kind natives, you might extrapolate that all Canadians are friendly.

Facetious

Treating serious issues with intentionally inappropriate humor; flippant.

Fallacious

Containing or based on incorrect reasoning; not correct.

Fastidious

Giving careful attention to detail; very attentive.

Flabbergasted

Feeling shocked or surprised, usually because of something unexpected.

Flummoxed

Completely unable to understand; so confused that you even do not know what to do (for example: Doctors were flummoxed by his symptoms).

Foible

Means a slight weakness in someone's character (for example: The minor foible in the woman's character made her unsuitable for the career she really wanted).

Fraudulent

Dishonest and illegal; false (for example: The police are investigating fraudulent claims).

Frenzy

Is a state or period of uncontrolled excitement or wild behavior. Frenzy is often used when talking about a group of people (or animals) who get worked up at the same time about the same thing.

Fret

Be constantly or visibly worried or anxious (for example: She spent the day fretting about that contact).

Frugal

Means thrifty, cheap; simple and plain and costing little.

Frustration

Can be described as the feeling of being upset or annoyed as a result of being unable to change or achieve something. There are two types of frustration: internal and external. Internal frustration may arise from challenges in fulfilling personal goals, desires, instinctual drives and needs, or dealing with perceived deficiencies, such as a lack of confidence or fear of social situations. External causes of frustration involve conditions outside an individual's control.

Galvanize

Means to shock or affect someone enough to produce a strong and immediate reaction, typically into taking action.

Gangling

Unusually tall and thin; not able to move gracefully.

Gestalt

Something that has particular qualities when you consider it as a whole which is not obvious when you consider only the separate parts of it.

Gluttonous

Means a person who eats or consumes immoderate amounts of food and drink; excessively greedy.

Grandiloquent

Style or way of using language in very complex way, in order to attract admiration and attention; big words used in a overly self-assured way.

Gregarious

Sociable; living in flocks or herds, as animals. A gregarious person enjoys being with other people.

Gullible

Easily persuaded to believe something (for example: TV Advertising tries to persuade a gullible audience to spend their money).

Hackneyed

Means something cliche that has been overused or done too much.

Harangue

Means speak with someone, often for a long time, with the use of force, especially in order to convince them.

Haughty

Means arrogant and condescending. When you're haughty, you have a big attitude and you behave as if you are better than others.

Hectic

Full of activity, or very busy and fast.

Hitherto

Means up to this point; until the present time.

Ignominious

Deserving or bringing disgrace or shame. If you describe an experience or action as ignominious, you mean it is embarrassing.

Impecunious

Having little or no money (for example: A titled but impecunious royal family).

Impetuous

Means rash, impulsive, acting without thinking.

Implementation

Is the process of putting a decision or plan into effect.

Impregnable

Resistant to capture or penetration; strong enough to resist or withstand attack; not to be taken by force. If you describe a building or other place as impregnable, you mean that it cannot be broken into or captured.

Inauguration

Is the act of putting a service, system, etc. into action, or an occasion when this happens.

Incensed

Angered at something unjust or wrong (for example: Teacher was incensed at his lack of concentration).

Inchoate

Not completely developed or clear. If something is inchoate, it is new or not yet properly developed.

Inconsequential

Unimportant, trivial (for example: His work seems trivial and inconsequential).

Indelible

Not able to be removed or erased. An example of indelible is ink that cannot be washed out of a shirt.

Indigenous

Indigenous people or things belong to the country in which they are found, rather than coming there from another country.

Indolent

Wanting to avoid activity or exertion; lazy, slothful.

Indubitable

Means something that cannot be doubted (for example: An indubitable fact).

Inept

Not skilled; generally incompetent and ineffective.

Inexorable

Incapable of being persuaded or placated; continuing without any possibility of being stopped.

Inevitable

Certain to happen and unable to be avoided or prevented.

Infatuation

A foolish and usually extravagant passion or love.

Infuse

Means to instill a quality of; to fill someone or something with an emotion or quality; add scent or flavor by steeping ingredients in it.

Initiation

(from Latin initium (meaning "entrance or beginning")) is a rite of passage marking entrance or acceptance into a group or society.

Inscrutable

Impossible to understand or interpret.

Insinuate

To say something which seems to mean something unpleasant without saying it openly; to suggest indirectly or subtly.

Insurgent

A rebel or revolutionary; in opposition to a civil authority or government.

Interpolation

Is an interruption or an addition inserted into something spoken or written. If you tell a story and then add some new parts, those are interpolations.

Intervention

Is an orchestrated attempt by one or many people - usually family and friends - to get someone to seek professional help with an addiction or some kind of traumatic event or crisis, or other serious problem; when a group of friends gets together to help out another friend who has a problem, like drugs, manic depression, beating his wife, etc. usually involves an informal get-together during which the friends all sit down and talk with the person having problems.

Intransigent

Refusing to compromise, often on an extreme opinion (for example: The company is intransigent and rejects any notion of a settlement).

Intrepid

(from Latin intrepidus, formed from the prefix in (not) + trepidus (alarmed)) - extremely brave and showing no fear of dangerous situations; fearless; adventurous (often used for rhetorical or humorous effect).

Inveterate

Habitual; someone who does something very often.

Invigorating

Making one feel strong and full of energy (for example: An invigorating swim).

Jaded

Bored or lacking enthusiasm, typically because you have experienced something too many times.

Jejune

Understanding or describing something in a way that is too simple, naive, or simplistic.

Jibe

Means an insulting or aggressive remark directed at a person and intended to have a telling effect.

Jubilation

Is a feeling of great happiness, triumph or joy (as winning competition).

Juxtaposition

Means two things placed beside each other for the sake of implicit comparison.

Laudable

Deserving praise and commendation. Laudable refers to something or someone who does the right thing or the morally proper action.

Leverage

Means getting an advantage. Leverage is the ability to influence situations or people so that you can control what happens (for example: His function as a boss affords him the leverage to get things done).

Liaise

Means to speak to people in other organizations in order to exchange information with them; to cooperate on a matter of mutual concern (for example: Our sales team liaise with the suppliers to ensure fast delivery).

Lobbying

Is the act of trying to persuade governments to make decisions or support something. Lobbying can be done by many sorts of people, alone or in groups. These people are called lobbyists.

Loquacious

Talking or tending to talk a great deal or freely; talkative; garrulous.

Ludicrous

So foolish, stupid, unreasonable, or inappropriate as to be amusing; ridiculous.

Lucid

Very clear and easy to understand (for example: He gave a clear and lucid report).

Maddening

Means extremely annoying or displeasing (for example: She has a maddening habit of interrupting other people).

Malaise

Uncertain or unfocused feeling of mental anxiety, illness, or discomfort.

Maverick

An independent person who has ideas and behaviour that are very different from other people's; one who resists adherence to a group.

Mediocre

Not very good; of average quality and you think it should be better (for example: The acting in this film is mediocre).

Memorandum

Is a short written report prepared specially for a person or group of people that contains information about a particular matter.

Mendacious

Lying; not telling the truth (for example: Mendacious propaganda).

Mercurial

Characterized by rapid change or temperament; sudden or unpredictable changes of mood or mind.

Metaphor

Is a figure of speech that directly refers to one thing by mentioning another for rhetorical effect. It does not use a word in its basic literal sense. Instead, it uses a word in a kind of comparison.

"I beat him with a stick" - literal meaning of "beat".

"I beat him in an argument" - metaphorical meaning of "beat".

Mettle

Means a person's ability to cope well with difficulties; strong-willed.

Modicum

A small quantity of a particular thing (for example: I was pleased with the overall response and I think we collectively felt a modicum of relief).

Mundane

Means ordinary, commonplace. Something that is mundane is very ordinary and not at all interesting or unusual. In subcultural and fictional uses, it is a person who does not belong to a particular group, according to the members of that group.

Mutter

To talk indistinctly, usually in a low voice (for example: She muttered something under his breath).

Negligence

Carelessness; failure to take proper care over something.

Nomenclature

Is a system of names or terms, or the rules for forming these terms in a particular field of arts or sciences. In other words, nomenclature is a system for giving names to things within a particular profession or field.

Nonchalant

Calm, casual, seeming unexcited; behaving in a calm manner, often in a way that suggests you are not interested or do not care.

Non sequitur

Is a statement that does not logically follow what has been said before (for example: It's time to take my car in for service. I wonder if my stylist is available this Tuesday).

Obfuscation

Is the act or an instance of making something obscure, dark, or difficult to understand; the obscuring of the intended meaning of a communication by making the message difficult to understand, usually with confusing and ambiguous language.

Obloquy

Is a censure, blame, or abusive language aimed at a person or thing, especially by numerous persons or by the society.

Obsequious

Attempting to win favor from influential people by flattery.

Obstreperous

Noisy, aggressive, and difficult to control (for example: Obstreperous customer; obstreperous drunk passenger on plane).

Opaque

Not able to be seen through; not easily understood. Use the adjective opaque either for something that doesn't allow light to pass through (like a heavy curtain) or for something difficult to understand.

Opulent

Wealthy; rich; ostentatiously costly and luxurious.

Ostentation

Is a show of something such as money, power, or skill that is intended to impress people.

Outbreak

Is a sudden occurrence of something unwelcome, such as war or disease. This term most commonly used in epidemiology. When more cases of a disease than expected are recorded in one area an outbreak is declared.

Outlier

Means an extreme deviation from the mean; a person, thing, or fact that is so different that can't be used for general conclusions.

Overt

Open and observable; not secret or concealed; done or shown publicly.

Oxymoron

Is a combination of two words used together that have, or seem to have, opposite meanings. Some examples of an oxymoron: Great Depression; cruel to be kind; painfully beautiful; alone together; wise fool; true myth, etc.

Paradigm

Is a model of something, or a very clear and typical example of something; a distinct set of concepts or thought patterns, including theories, research methods, postulates, and standards for what constitutes legitimate contributions to a field.

Parched

Shriveled; dried out because of too much heat and not enough rain.

Parsimonious

Excessively unwilling to spend (for example: The director of that company was very parsimonious, so he decided not to expand the staff).

Peremptory

Speaking or behaving rudely, as if you expect other people to obey/submit you immediately and without any questions.

Perfidious

Faithless, disloyal, untrustworthy. If you describe someone as perfidious, you mean that they have betrayed someone or cannot be trusted.

Perfunctory

Means something done without much care or attention; done quickly, without much interest.

Perpetual

Continuing forever or indefinitely; never ending or changing.

Perseverance

Means persistence in doing something despite the difficulties.

Pert

Characterized by a lightly saucy or impudent quality; one who is not afraid to say what's on his mind.

Placate

Means to make (someone) less angry or hostile; to appease or pacify, especially by concessions or conciliatory gestures.

Plethora

Means a very large amount of something, especially a larger amount than you need, want, or can deal with.

Postulate

Means something assumed without proof as being self-evident or generally accepted, especially when used as a basis for an argument; a fundamental element; a basic principle. Sometimes postulates are not obviously correct, but are required for their consequences.

Prattle

Means to talk in a silly way for a long time about things that are not important or without saying anything important.

Preamble

(from the Latin praeambulum (meaning "walking before")) is an introductory statement in a document that explains the document's purpose and underlying philosophy, and clarifies the meaning of the operative part of the text in case of an ambiguity or dispute.

Precipitate

Means to make something happen quickly, suddenly or sooner than expected.

Preponderance

Exceeding in heaviness; the largest part or greatest amount. If there's a preponderance of something, there is a lot of it.

Presumption

Is the act of believing that something is true without having any proof. In the law of evidence, a presumption of a particular fact can be made without the aid of proof in some situations.

Prevaricate

Means to avoid telling the truth by not directly answering a question.

Proclamation

Is a public announcement about something important.

Prostration

Is the placement of the body in a reverentially or submissively prone position as a gesture; the action of lying with the face down and arms stretched out, especially as a sign of respect or worship.

Protract

Lengthen in time; cause to be or last longer. If you have a disagreement with a friend that you continue for days, you are protracting the argument.

Prowl

Means to move about in or as if in a predatory manner.

Prudent

Careful, cautious; avoiding risks.

Puerile

Behaving in a silly way; childish.

Pugnacious

Aggressive, ready to argue or fight with people.

Quaff

Means to swallow hurriedly or greedily or in one draught (for example: He quaffed pint after pint of good German beer).

Quench

To slake, satisfy, or allay (thirst, desires, passion, etc.). For example, if you quench your thirst, you drink something so that you no longer feel thirsty.

Querulous

Often complaining; irritable. A querulous person complains often and in a way that irritate (annoys) other people.

Quid pro quo

(from Latin "this for that") means giving something in exchange for getting something; a favour or advantage granted in return for something.

Quintessence

Is the most typical example of something. For example, the Parthenon in Greece was considered the quintessence of the perfectly proportioned building.

Quixotic

Hopeful or romantic in a way that is extremely idealistic; unrealistic and impractical.

Ramification

Means possible results of an action. The ramifications of a decision or event are all its consequences and effects, especially ones which are not obvious at first.

Rancorous

Means hateful. A rancorous argument or person is full of bitterness and anger.

Reclusive

Preferring to live in isolation; avoiding the company of other people.

Recondite

Means something that is difficult or impossible for most to understand, or that most people don't know about.

Redundant

Not or no longer needed or useful; unnecessary because it is more than is needed (for example: The company made hundreds of employees redundant).

Refurbish

Renovate and redecorate something; improve the appearance or functionality of.

Refute

Prove to be wrong or false; overthrow by argument, evidence, or proof.

Reiterate

Means to say, state, or perform something again or a number of times, usually for emphasis or clarity.

Relativism

Is an idea that views are relative to differences in perception and consideration. There is no universal, objective truth according to relativism; rather each point of view has its own truth.

Remorse

Deep regret or guilt for a wrong committed.

Repudiate

Refuse to accept, acknowledge, ratify, or recognize as valid.

Resilient

Able to withstand or recover quickly from difficult conditions; bounce back.

Rubicon

Is a point of no return; to cross/pass the Rubicon means to take a decisive, irrevocable step.

Sacrosanct

Holy, something that should not be criticized.

Sanctum

A sacred place, especially a shrine within a temple or church.

Sardonic

Means a disdainfully or ironically humorous; scornful, cynical and mocking.

Schism

Division of a group into opposing factions. When there is a schism, a group or organization divides into two groups as a result of differences in thinking and beliefs.

Scintillating

Means something brilliantly and excitingly clever or skilful; fascinating.

Scrupulous

Characterized by extreme care and great effort; extremely attentive to details; very concerned to avoid doing wrong.

Scrutinize

To look at something very closely or very carefully (for example: The evidence was carefully scrutinized).

Serendipity

Means an occurrence and development of events by chance in a happy or beneficial way (for example: A fortunate stroke of serendipity).

Shatter

Means to break suddenly into very small pieces, or to make something break in this way.

Smuggling

If someone smuggles things or people into a place or out of it, they take them there illegally or secretly.

Spurious

Means plausible but false; not being what it purports to be; fake.

Stalemate

Means a situation in which it seems impossible to settle an argument or disagreement, and neither side can get an advantage.

Status quo

Is a Latin phrase meaning the existing state of affairs, particularly with regard to social or political issues. In the sociological sense, it generally applies to maintain or change existing social structure and values.

Strident

Means unpleasantly loud and harsh (for example: Her voice had become increasingly strident).

Supplicant

Is a person who asks someone who is in a position of power for something in a very humble way. If you pray every night to be accepted to your dream college, you can call yourself a supplicant.

Synecdoche

Is a figure of speech in which a part is made to represent the whole or vice versa. If you buy a car and you say to your friends that you just got a new set of wheels, you're using synecdoche - you're using the wheels, which are part of a car, to refer to the whole car ("a pair of hands" is a synecdoche for "a worker"; "the law" for "a police officer").

Taboo

Is a vehement prohibition of an action based on the belief that such behavior is either too sacred or too accursed for ordinary individuals to undertake.

Taciturn

Means uncommunicative. Someone who is taciturn does not speak often and does not say very much.

Tatty

Old and in bad condition (for example: The stairs looked a bit tatty for a house which has been open only for a few days).

Tautology

Is the use of different words to say the same thing twice in the same statement. The word tautology is derived from the Greek word tauto (meaning "the same") and logos (meaning "a word or an idea"). For example, "They spoke in turn, one after the other" is considered a tautology because "in turn" and "one after the other" mean the same thing.

Teeming

Abundantly filled or swarming with something, as with people (for example: The Internet is teeming with viruses).

Tenacious

Determined to do something and unwilling to stop trying even when the situation becomes difficult, keeping a firm grip on.

Tentative

Not definite; not certain or fixed (for example: tentative report; tentative verdict; etc.).

Tenuous

Having little substance or strength; unsure; weak (for example: Police have only found a tenuous connection between the two murders).

Terrestrial

Of or relating to the earth or its inhabitants. An example of a terrestrial is a person who lives on the planet.

Transcendental

Literally means beyond the limits of cognition and earthly experience. Transcendental describes anything that has to do with the spiritual, non-physical world.

Trepidation

Means a feeling of fear, alarm, or anxiety about something that may happen.

Ubiquitous

Found everywhere; omnipresent. If you describe something or someone as ubiquitous, you mean that they seem to be everywhere.

Underlie

Be the cause or basis of something (for example: What really underlies most heart disease?).

Unkempt

Not properly maintained or cared for (for example: His hair was unkempt and dirty).

Utilitarianism

Is the system of thought which states that the best action or decision in a particular situation is the one that brings more advantages to the most people.

Vacillate

Means to waver between different opinions or actions.

Vagabonding

Means someone who wanders from place to place and has no home or job.

Verisimilitude

Being believable, or having the appearance of being true (for example: You can improve your game by using the real sounds of the ocean, to create verisimilitude).

Vicarious

Experienced as a result of watching, listening to, or reading about the activities of other people, rather than by doing the activities yourself (for example: Lots of people use television as their vicarious form of social life).

Vicissitude

Is a change of circumstances or fortune, typically one that is unwanted or unpleasant.

Vilify

Spread negative information about something or someone (for example: She has been vilified in the press).

Vindicate

To clear from an accusation, suspicion or criticism (for example: If he can vindicate his client of the charges he will be performing a miracle).

Vitriolic

Harsh, bitter, or malicious in tone. Vitriolic language or behaviour is cruel and full of hate.

Volatile

Likely to change rapidly and unpredictably; unstable; varying frequently between extreme highs and lows (for example: A volatile person can suddenly become angry or violent).

Wanton

Undisciplined, lustful. A wanton action deliberately causes harm, damage, or waste without having any reason to.

Watershed

Literally means a region of land within which water flows down into a specified body; but also describes a critical point that marks a division or a change of course; a turning point.

Wry

Humorously sarcastic or mocking; showing that you think something is funny but not very pleasant, often by the expression on your face.

Zeal

Is a strong feel of interest and enthusiasm that makes someone very eager or determined to do something (Zealous - filled with eagerness in pursuit of something).

Zeugma

Is the use of a word to modify or govern two or more words usually in such a manner that it applies to each in a different sense or makes sense with only one (for example: She broke his car and his heart; He opened his mind and his wallet at the movies; He fished for compliments and for trout).

From authors:

We hope this book will be useful in your C2 preparation. In order to remember as many definitions as possible and take the maximum from this material, we recommend you:

1) Fully read this book at least 2-3 times;

2) Write down for yourself the definitions that you remember better and learn them first;

3) After that, learn 3-5 words a day, every day.

We wish you the best of luck, your CEP Publishing Team.

CPSIA information can be obtained
at www.ICGtesting.com
Printed in the USA
BVHW060402100620
581183BV00008B/571